Bradford Cox

Sadalpha

A Voyage of Life

Bradford Cox

Sadalpha
A Voyage of Life

ISBN/EAN: 9783744652520

Printed in Europe, USA, Canada, Australia, Japan

Cover: Foto ©Andreas Hilbeck / pixelio.de

More available books at **www.hansebooks.com**

SADALPHA;

OR

A VOYAGE OF LIFE.

BY

J. BRADFORD COX, M. D.

SAN JOSE, CAL.

1880.
MERCURY STEAM PRINT
SAN JOSE.

Entered according to Act of Congress in the year 1879, by J. B. Cox, in the Office of the Librarian of Congress at Washington.

PREFACE.

In presenting this little book for publication the author is aware of many of its deficiencies. But with a hope that it may be the means of exciting a desire for a more perfect life than many people now live, and that it may afford pleasure during its perusal, indulgence is craved for its imperfections.

A recent criticism on the "Poetry of the Familiar," in a leading literary journal, seems to express the tendency of poetic taste at present in the following words: "In this art movement we see just what has been going on in poetry and fiction. Poets and romancists began by believing that only romantic and picturesque scenes were worthy of their muse. They delighted in the supernatural; in the impossible, remote and extravagant; in the grand, heroic and appalling. But we all know how the romantic gradually shifted into the merely picturesque, and then the picturesque into the familiar, until at last it has been discovered that even the most homely scenes and objects often possess every attribute of poetry."

This poem contains nothing supernatural, impossible, remote or appalling; and if the scenes and incidents portrayed fall short of the beautiful, or fail to entertain, it is altogether the fault of an inexperienced pen.

That there is much beauty in scenes of every day life is beyond doubt an established fact. And if we do not see and perceive it the fault lies in the instruction of our eyes and minds rather than in the scenes themselves. J. B. C.

SAN JOSE, Cal., Oct. 11th, 1879.

"What though we may not turn again
  To shores of childhood that we leave—
Are those old signs we followed vain ?
  Can guides so oft found true deceive ?

"Oh, sail we to the south or north,
  Oh, sail we to the east or west,
The port from which we first put forth
  Is our heart's home— is our life's best."

I DEDICATE THESE PAGES

TO THE MEMORY OF ONE WHOSE MORAL EXCELLENCE

LARGELY CONTRIBUTED TO THEIR PRODUCTION; WHOSE RELIGIOUS

LIFE WAS ONE OF BEAUTY AND CONSISTENCY; AND WHO OFTEN EXPRESSED A DESIRE

TO DO SOMETHING MORE TO BENEFIT MANKIND.   THIS BRIEF POEM

IS OFFERED AS A PART OF THE FRUIT OF HER

SHORT, THOUGH WELL SPENT LIFE.

Part 1.

INTRODUCTION.

FAR out upon the western point of land,
 Where calm Pacific throws her loving arms
 About the neck of Mendocino's Cape,
Whose rocky brow seems pleased for this embrace,
 Stood youthful Angus with his flowing hair
Kissed by the breeze, that played a hymn of praise
Among the rolling billows, and the rocks
Its constant harp. The soul-inspiring scene
Now charms his inexperienced, tender mind,
And transports thought beyond the narrow range
Of childhood's home, or youthful fancy's dream.

He sees, as 'twere, immensity of space
Spread out before him in the rolling deep,
And wonders what its depths may now contain.
He little knows, so young—scarce nineteen years—
The mysteries of its deep and hidden bed.
                Much less he knows
How great the commerce of her mighty ships.
And now he sees upon the vast expanse,
Far out from land as almost lost from view,
In midst of boundless deep, a whitened sail.
He wonders not of what its mission be:
If trade with foreign lands, he knows it not:
If plunder, piracy perchance its aim,
He thinks not of the dark and bloody deeds
Its crew may oft have done. He sees alone
The placid beauty of the tranquil scene.
'Tis Nature's voice that now he hears and heeds;

She speaks in varied tone to his young heart.

Beneath his feet the surging billows roar

And beat against the everlasting hills

And rocks, as they for cycles now have done;

Thus making thorough bass for all the songs

And melodies which Nature here can sing.

'Tis deep and loud enough for many tunes

That form a beauteous medley, speaking forth

The voice of Nature since the morning stars

Sang first their glorious hymn of love and praise.

The song that now he hears, as pensively

He sits him down 'mid ferns and waving grass,

Is one whose melody the sea-birds make,

Now high and shrill above the alto tones

Of various tribes of anseres floating near;

While from the many rocks not far away

Comes forth the tenor and the second bass

From out the throats of hundreds of the race
Of lions, seals, as they come forth to warm
Their shining backs beneath the noonday sun;
While constantly deep organ tones, from rocks
And rolling waves, fill up and bear on high
The perfect harmony.

          He listens more attentively:
The voices vary as he hears each tone
Express a something more than music sweet.
A feeling, a desire, perchance a thought
Leaps forth with each distinct and separate tone
Of this grand chorus of the mighty deep.
Loud and strong it now bursts forth
In animated strains, that seem to say
All Nature joins in one glad hymn of praise.
And then a cadence seems to come, and short
Staccato tones, with their untold surprise,

Blend sweetly into other strains that move;

Allegro maestoso, which now bring

A striving for a great and noble end

Within that breast which their grand import feels.

And now a modulation seems to come

Adagio, in a mournful minor key,

And with it sad reflections o'er the past.

   He turns to view the land.

Far to the east extends in Rainbow form

A Ridge with green and smooth and grassy top;

With gently convex surface to the north:

Its lower border fringed with cañons deep,

Made dark and wild by dense and sombre growth

Of firs and pines, madronas and liveoaks;

Amid whose cool inviting shades wild deer

And grouse and California lions find

A safe retreat. Far in the distant east

Mount up great snow-capped peaks which seem to say,
The farther up from earth we raise our heads
The purer and more peaceful we become.
The hoary-headed parents seem they now
Of all their varied loving progeny—
The smaller peaks uplifting verdant heads.
What hundreds of these children have they borne
And scattered here and there, until they seem
A vast assembled throng of human heads.
Perchance they now in awe and reverence stand,
As youth before a hoary-headed sire,
To hear what lessons come from wisdom's lips.
Hark! hear a sage with whitened locks,
In tones so deep that all the throng may hear,
Speak forth and say, as father to a child,
Once on a time, far down in early years,
Before mankind was known upon the earth,

When I was young and in my youthful prime,
Then you had first your birth. Centuries your heads
Scarce peeped above the briny, rolling deep,
Which dashed its surging breakers ceaselessly
About my isolated form.
   Then life came forth
And made abode upon my barren sides.
Then, too, within the midst of impure deep
Began to teem still other life, until
When you emerged above the water's waste
This life in all its forms seemed everywhere
Itself to reproduce.
By slow degrees, through cycles dim and long,
By fires that burned within my throbbing breast,
I grew to manhood's prime.
You, my first born, long I watched
Amid the surging billows, which at times

Would near submerge you from my anxious sight.

How long, how long, I can not tell how long,

Ere man came forth to dwell upon us here.

To me the time since first he came to us

Seems but a moment of my life.

He comes and goes much like the tender grass

That decks your verdant brows.

Young Angus shuddered as he heard this voice

Concerning that of which he formed a part.

He wondered if indeed the sage be wise.

He fain would know what else may be in man

Besides the vital force that makes him grow

In stature as the living grass or tree.

He looks within his inmost soul and finds

A thirst for wisdom, which is never quenched,

Except he drink from out the purest fount.

Oh, Wisdom, infinite, he cries aloud,

Give me to drink that I may thirst no more!
He turns to mingle with his fellow man,
And ask of him, if this be all of life?
He watches man from early dawn of love
To its fruition, happiness and peace:
Till death comes on to claim its own 'mid tears,
And weeping, bleeding hearts that know no rest.
And then he turns and asks the hoary sage,
If life be ended when we cease to live?

PREPARATION.

BEHOLD two tender loving souls,
   'Mid joy and mirth and glee,
   While showers of blessing love controls
Sail forth on life's rough sea.

Oh, what will be their doubtful fate?
   What storms—what calms be theirs?
How reach their port? too soon? too late?
   In answer to what prayers?

Shall joy attend them on their way?
   Shall grief be theirs? Who knows?
Shall peace crown evening every day?
   And sweet be their repose?

O. happy trusting pair, to be
    Thus joined in heart and hand!
How gladly friends give speed to thee,
    While watching from the strand!

Their boat steers proudly for the main,
    And friends with voices clear
Repeat the joyous, glad refrain.
    " Long life to them—so dear."

This sea of life they soon will prove,
    Not one which ever bears
All placid scenes and ships that move
    As smoothly on as theirs!

Each happy in the other's love,
    They feast, they drink deep bliss;
They revel as blest souls above
    And all seems joy like this.

Oh, happy, joyous, loving pair!
    No stain of sin now mars
Your highest ecstacy; for prayer
    Brought pardon from the stars.

Each sought the Savior years agone,
    And pardoned through His blood,
They strived to live as He alone
    Has ordered in His Word.

How oft they failed He surely knew,
    For penitent each came
At eventide, and meekly through
    The power, in Jesus' name,

Begged mercy for the sinning soul
    And wisdom from on high;
And as the days and years might roll
    That He would be near by;

That His own presence would be near
    In every act and word,
And heart be kept as fountain clear
    That moves but is not heard.

With hearts thus pure they first had met
    At feast of intellect,
Where teachers Joint Convention set,
    To plan how best to act.

To venture on some new laid plan
    Of how to train the mind;
And thus by lifting youthful man
    To benefit mankind.

To talk of methods and of rules,
    Of aspirations bright,
Of how to manage country schools
    And train the youth aright.

They talked these matters o'er and o'er,
    And much that appertained
To other things than those of lore
    And how the youth be trained.

They talked of nature and of flowers,
    Surrounding lakes and trees,
Of valleys fair, and leisure hours,
    Of life—its stormy seas.

And when the sessions daily closed,
    And lunch and dinner o'er,
A horseback ride was then proposed
    And taken as before:

Through vales, o'er hills, 'mid pine woods sweet,
    By gushing springs so clear:
Now manzanita blossoms greet,
    Nor leaf is brown and sear.

For joyous Springtime with its flowers,
    Bedecking bush and lawn,
Invites to wild and perfumed bowers
    As evening shades come on.

Thus pleasantly the time was passed:
    The three days' session done;
A store of knowledge was amassed
    As how the school should run;

As how this one and that had tried
    The boisterous to restrain;
How indolence was rectified
    And duty made quite plain.

Thus interchanging thoughts the while
    Of work and labor true,
They learned to love;—the time beguile
    As youthful lovers do.

They talked of Springtime, hopes and gains,
    Of usefulness and toil,
When coming years should crown their pains
    With harvest of the soil.

They sowed good seed, then why not wait
    Till harvest time should come,
And gather sheaves both small and great,
    Rewards of work well done?

The future seemed all bright and fair,
    Nor clouds athwart their sky;
Buoyant of soul, a hopeful pair,
    No tear to dim the eye.

For weeks—yea, months—this pleasure ran—
    Delightful stream of love;
God's providence approved the plan
    And sanctioned from above.

Not spoken love—at first quite dim;
   So timid, half afraid;
Then "sister would she be to him,"
   How sweet first promise made!

A "sister," but "no more!"—Just here
   A "brother's love" was pledged:
"I'll take you as my 'sister dear'
   Till fuller love be fledged."

But sickness came, the manly form
   Was stricken near to death;
For days and weeks contagion's storm
   Raged o'er him with its breath.

A much loved letter sent away
   To her, from his sick room,
In distant home drove friends astray
   For fear infection's doom.

She read it through, how anxiously
　　None else but she could tell;
A peaceful thought came hopefully
　　That "brother" might get well.

When convalescence scarce was o'er,
　　Proud Science for his aim,
He leaves the bright Pacific shore
　　To seek and delve for fame.

With fond farewells from all his friends,
　　And "sisters" too, save one,
He bids adieu to seek amends
　　For ravages just done.

Goes anxiously, with sad regret,
　　At leaving thus her face,
Whose image hovered round him yet
　　And lingered at the place

Where fevered fancy oft had gone,
    Through mountains green and fair.
By many a gurgling stream sat down,
    That face was ever there.

And even when in death's embrace,
    So near that few came by,
His deep delirium saw that face
    With pity in its eye.

He called her oft in loving tone,
    He whispered that sweet name;
Attendants heard him--heard him moan,
    And wondered if she came.

She came in spirit, not in form;
    She came and soothed him so;
She banished all the loathsome storm
    And cleansed him pure as snow.

In fancy thus he traversed o'er
    Bright scenes, where months ago,
In respite from their work of lore
    They loved so oft to go.

But recollections such as these,
    From well or fevered brain,
Proved recompense, to somewhat ease
    The parting and its pain.

To recollect these happier times,
    To travel once again
By lake and stream, whose murmuring chimes
    Wrote music without pen;

To walk again through pine woods sweet,
    To climb the mountain's brow,
To wander where the waters meet,
    Seemed dear to him just now.

For in the busy city's strife,
    The Golden Gate so nigh,
He walks alone, though surging life
    Is hurrying, rustling by.

He visits places then of note,
    He sees and is not seen;
So small a thing, a useless mote,
    A something which has been.

A person, living, thinking, loved,
    A consciousness, of what?
Of having been, of having moved
    Around one little spot!

Of having loved one beauteous face,
    Distinct from all seen now.
O, could it come from out its place,
    With pure and noble brow,

And penetrate this jostling crowd,
    And turn its eyes toward me,
How sweet 'twould be with step so proud
    To walk and converse free!

O, could not this one boon be given,
    To see her ere he start?
'Twould be to him foretaste of Heaven
    To embrace before they part.

But no! to-morrow brings the day
    On which his vessel sails
For Panama; and he must say
    His farewell through the mails.

That night he wrote, ah, yes, how well
    None else but she could know!
Emotions deep the bosom swell,
    A heaving to and fro

Of love and hope, of doubt and fear,
    Uncertainty and grief.
Oh, could e'en present be made clear
    'Twould bring the soul relief.

" This life has much in store for me;
    Much more than I now see
Can come through my scant lore to me.
    I'm now unworthy thee.

" So when I've climbed the giddy hight,
    And wrought in science' dome,
Will my dear sister to me write,
    And welcome letters home

" From her dear brother far away?
    If so my task will be
Made light indeed, and on my way
    I'll write, oft write to thee."

Part 2.

ON THE PACIFIC.

Out on the ocean wave sailing along;
Why should I not now change my song?
Steady the billows roll, oh, so high!
Steady the heart sends sigh after sigh.

Chasing each other the waves come on;
Chasing each other the faces now gone
Come in remembrance to sadden the scene;
Thus to be leaving them;—Oh, how keen

Breaks out the anguish from the depths of the soul!
Break up the crested waves as inward they roll;
Break up glad scenes of home—now they come near;
Break up old friendships so long held dear;
Breaks up the rocky beach?   O! no, no!
Firmly it withstands the tides high or low.
Breaks up a "sister's love?"   Oh! no, no!
Breaks up a "brother's love?"   No! surely no!
Firmly they withshand the rolling of the tide,
The busy throng that jostles round on every side.
Sailing on the ocean—the calm Pacific fair,
Now away from breakers--scarce a breath of air.
Rolling now the rollers, Oh, so slowly on!
Coming not from stormy climes; coming, coming, gone!
Noiselessly they come and go, ever rolling high!
Ship's machinery humming keeps time with hearts'
   lone sigh.

All quietness and grandeur!
    Save sailors here and there,
Preparing for the voyage,
    Dead stillness fills the air.

The breakers far behind us,
    The land grows dim to view,
Thus seeming to remind us
    Of friendships fond and true;

Of faces in the distance
    That seem to say farewell;
Of many scenes and incidents
    That now the heart do spell,

And bind us to the fading shore
    That soon will disappear.
The faces loved in days of yore
    Seem now to be more dear,

As memory turns to view again
   Loved places where we trod,
And recollect on hill in glen
   Bright scenes spread out where God

Would draw the soul toward Him again
   From whom it wanders oft—
Yes, wanders into hell's dark den
   Until it may be lost.

Bright recollections of the past
   Come now the heart to thrill.
Sweet memories! yes, they come, how fast
   The soul the thoughts to fill!

Some come with gentle tread, and steal
   So soft, so quietly,
Upon our musings that we feel
   Their impress peacefully.

Some come with longings to return
  And be again with those
Whose love now follows every turn
  Our wandering feet may choose.

Some bring a sigh for misspent time,
  But others bring relief;
Some bring a joy, while others chime
  The deep-toned bells of grief.

Oh! happy, peaceful, pensive hour,
  Thy moments come and go
As sunshine bright or April shower,
  Summer's heat or Winter's snow!

Some moments freeze the tender heart
  Toward all mankind; so cold,
So selfishly, each acts his part
  That many things untold

Are treasured in the inmost soul,
  And there deep hidden lay;
But now our memories o'er them roll
  And bring them bright as day

To re-enact the scenes gone by
  With all their joy and pain,
And vividly they come so nigh
  The present we disdain.

Thus musing till e'en past grew dim,
  His voyage just begun,
A well-known voice now greeted him.
  A hand was grasped by one

In former days a better heart,
  Whose vain attempt at wealth,
In mines as well as healing art,
  Had only brought poor health

Through dissipation long indulged,
    And now he seeks relief
From horrors—need they be divulged?
    Oh, demons sweet is grief

Compared to terror and suspense,
    Of madness from the bowl!
What pleasure that can recompense
    This torture of the soul?

Oh! man, why desecrate the mind?
    Why wallow in the mire,
And in damnation surely bind
    Thy soul to eternal fire?

He sought a reformation when,
    Through changes of the trip,
He should be made himself again
    By life on board the ship.

He has a fortune in the East,
 Some land, a rich estate,
Is left from father late deceased,
 Far in old Keystone State.

" But what brings you, so young," he said,
 " To leave the Golden State,
Where home and friends and much might aid
 A promise to be great?"

" Sir, this is why you see me go,"
 The youth at once replied;
" I've labored hard, as you may know,
 The money to provide

That I might fit myself to be
 Of use to fellow man,
Far more than in the school I see,
 Or working with the hand.

And so I've wrought most ardently
  These past three years or more,
And all my wages carefully
  Laid by in future store.

For this my trip to Bellvue Halls,
  Where I in time shall be
Prepared, like you, to attend the calls
  Of sick humanity."

' Ah! foolish youth!" the sage replied;
  " How strange your choice to me!
Far better for you had you died
  In early infancy,

Than thus to wear your life away
  At call of come who will,
And never know by night or day
  What hours repose shall fill.

Far better had you been content
    To teach a country school,
Where every moment is well spent
    And leisure comes by rule.

But since you go and can't turn back,
    Perhaps 'tis vain for me
To try dissuasion from the track
    Of pain and misery.

But when you've followed many years
    Disease and death and woe,
With all their ravages and tears,
    Perhaps you'll say 'tis so."

But say when did you leave the once fair mountain town,
With its adjacent hills and its valleys now brown?
And say, how are old friends and acquaintances there?

A VOYAGE OF LIFE.

And pray how your young "schoolma'am," so gay
    and so fair?
And how was your preceptor, the good Doctor D——,
Whose only great fault was a jolly good spree?
Thus oft they conversed as now onward they sailed.
When eating and sleeping and reading had failed;
Now pacing the deck that the time might go by,
Or watching alone for the wonders that lie
Far down in the depths of the fathomless sea,
So wonderful now for its transparency;
Often looking for land that was seldom now seen,
Or viewing the star depths, so calm and serene;
Now wondering how, from the expanse of Heaven,
The Ruler beholds our green earth as it's driven
Around our own sun, which to us seems so bright,
And yet from His Home is a mere speck of light.
How small is the earth when compared to these suns,

Which soften the darkness as night o'er earth runs!
Ah! vainly would we with our finite eyesight,
Were we placed at the centre of infinite light,
Endeavor to find such a planet as earth,
With its show and splendor, its seeming great worth.
Yet Infinite Wisdom views all He hath made,
The suns and the planets and satellites staid
Revolving so grandly, while each in its place
Permits every other its journey to trace
Without molestation, still influence is shed
By each on its neighbor, while surely they're led
In perfect accord with the Ruler's great plan,
Thus pointing a moral to weak, sinful man.
But onward for days, through the sunshine and rain,
The ship plows along o'er the blue, rolling main;
Now Lower California has come and has gone,
With its bold Cape St. Lucas, so clear in the dawn.

Manzanillo, its tempting and tropical sight,

Has left in the memory bright pictures of night.

With its bald though green hills as so snugly they lay

With light-house and cañons around the smooth bay.

But beautiful—aye, what a joy to behold it!

A sunset in Autumn with Him to unfold it,

Who is beauty itself, and who paints, oh, so bright,

That artists ne'er equal in visions of light!

A sunset on ocean, with tropical air

To bring forth each outline and make it more fair.

A scene to enjoy which the heart we must raise

To the source of all beauty and tune to His praise.

Such a scene was presented ere Panama gained.

The day had been showery; so oft had it rained

That sailors work scrubbing the deck was not needed,

Nor furling the sails, for this had preceded

Approach of the evening, which now coming on

Seemed hallowed, for Sabbath day now nearly gone
Brings its eve on so gently to mind ere it sleep,
Favoring silence and reverie and memories deep
Of childhood, of Springtime, of friends that are gone,
Of other scenes far away—how they come on!
Now flooding the soul as if dreamland were here
To carry us back over many a glad year.

REFLECTIONS.

PAINS quickly vanishing,
    Joys e'er replenishing,
        Ever surviving the brightest and best
        For man's true happiness,
        Pleasure and blessedness,
Resting in wisdom—how sweet is that rest!

    Past scenes come peacefully,
    Come they so quietly,
Thus are they filling the heart full of love.
    Coming now joyfully,
    Coming then tearfully,
Coming from whence are they? Ah! from above!

They from the soul seem welling—
Seem to the heart now telling
Sweetly and calmly of past times so dear.
Oh! how they thrill the heart!
May they not soon depart.
Stay, pleasant memories, ever stay near.

Stay to enrich the soul,
While round us billows roll—
Billows of turmoil from great human strife.
Hallowed thy influence be
O'er all life's stormy sea,
Never forsaking me through endless life.

A SUNSET.

BUT now behold!
　　In yonder western sky paints God a scene
　　　More beautiful than man has e'er beheld.
Or memories of artist e'er can paint.
No speech of earth can equal its portrayal.
Archways of cloud now rise in glorious light,
Resplendence all athwart the glowing sky.
Here northward mounts a mighty cumulus
On mountain range of other rolling clouds,
As bright as with the heat of incandescence.

They rise in range, beyond and over range,
And peaks still yet beyond, until away
In obscure distance, darkening shades of night,
There form befitting background to the scene;
While here and there are growing shadows as
Of valleys fair between the beauteous hills;
And then again of cañons deep that delve
And split the mountain sides.

   Wild with deep confusion,
And terrible with dark abysses that
Seem now to pierce the wondrous ocean's depths.
And yet so constantly a change comes o'er
That each new look brings forth new beauties.
Ah! ne'er was mountain scene like this!

   There southward lay more tranquil forms.
A stratus spreads far o'er the water's waste
And brings to view a second ocean calm,

With coasts and bays and wide expanse—it seems
'Twere hung in air. Its ships wax great then change
As if to mountains, quiet and serene.
Now rivers form and flow to distant shores,
Thus cheating fancy, which now sees instead
One vast and beauteous, changeful landscape fair,
With here and there small hills of doubtful green.
Ah! see again! beyond in distance dim
This phantom ocean spreads itself once more,
And soon again transforms to landscape bright,
With town and village interspersed; and broad
Highway still girt between, on which bright forms
Now move and pass, and slowly wax in size
Until great monsters to the sight they seem.

  And now behold the sinking sun
Half hidden in the deep—the centre piece
Of all this glorious scene—'mid gorgeous gates

And bright archways of cloud that multiply
To almost an infinitude of numbers.

   One grand triumphal archway
Spreads o'er him as he slowly disappears.
The bright blue sky beyond is only seen
Through his inviting open palace door.
While he in grandeur gently sinks from view
Amid this gorgeous beauty all around
He sheds new glory on still other scenes,
On other archways, architraves, and now
On golden stairs that lead to visions bright
And most profound. That lead in fancy bold
Beyond the darkness of the tomb into
The glorious mystery of the Home of God.

A SEQUEL TO THE SUNSET.

CLIMB now these stairways,
Pass through these doorways,
Walk through the palaces so beautifully bright,
View the many mansions,
So grand in dimensions,
Fountainebleau and Windsor equal not the sight.

Only this an emblem,
Only slight the semblance
To the grandeur of the real heavenly scene,
Where God in His glory
With Christ—O, blessed story!—
Now reigns in love and mercy so serene.

Here stands a gate ajar.

Come, oh, man, from afar
With holy awe and reverence enter thou in!

Remove first thy sandal,

Now again thy mantle,
For the place where thou standest knows no sin.

Thy faint heart that trembles

But slightly resembles
Those we shall meet with as onward we pass.

No shadows round us fall,

Light shines in all, through all,
Transparent every form as clear crystal glass.

Yet how distinct they seem!

Beauty—yes, the holy theme!
And mystery of mysteries how this can be.

Naught with the finite sight,

Naught though such radiant light
Could man distinguish where these forms we see.

Greater now the mystery,
Earth bears no history
Of like things and like scenes that now come on:
Inside the pearly gate
Come voices—oh, so sweet!—
Musical, angelic, in converse and in song.

A happy throng has gathered,
And by no sin now tethered.
They wander and enjoy whatsoe'er they will:
Their music sweet and perfect,
Their voices speak seraphic,
While joy and bliss ecstatic their souls now thrill.

Here come happy faces
From out celestial places,

More beautiful than ever known to earth.

    The faces, how resplendent!

    Their joy beams out transcendent,

So happy now since death brought their new birth.

    Well-known voices greet us,

    Loving eyes now meet us

With joy to know,—-so glad to see us come.

    Outstretched arms enfold us,

    Long they love to hold us.

O! the rapture of our own future home!

    You've come to stay forever,

    For here no partings sever

Us who reach this blissful place so bright.

    Our home is so delightful,

    There's nothing here despiteful,

All is love and purity for God is the light.

So glad you've come, my darling;

How sad it was our parting,

When death came to our circle down below!

But did you know then, dearest,

Your trial seemed severest,

That I would come to meet you when you'd go?

PANAMA.

MID contemplations such as these
   The night drew slowly on,
With not a rppie, not a breeze,
   To roll the waves along.

Old Panama now nearly gained,
   From which some news to send,
Of journey prospered, distance gained,
   And how the time to spend,

Found utterance in the ink and pens
    Laid by for times of need;
And now he writes to many friends,
    He writes his time to speed.

He writes again and still the same,
    The first lines seem not meet
For one whose memory ever came
    As "sister's love" more sweet.

Blue sky reflected in the deep
    Seems constantly to say,
Your image I as surely keep
    When you are far away

As ocean holds to wondering man
    A mirror of the skies,
Reflecting also God's own plan
    Before astonished eyes.

If constantly the sky be blue
　　Then ocean so appears;
If clouds obscure, the mirror true
　　Brings darkness, stormy fears.

So love from deep within the heart
　　Reflects most constantly
What it may feel to form a part
　　Of loved one's purity.

Yet Panama so near to view
　　Still must be many an hour,
For slow the smoke and steam now flew,
　　The engine lost its power.

So slowly moves the mighty craft
　　That something seems amiss,
A floating, lifeless, aimless raft,
　　Anxiety like this,

A VOYAGE OF LIFE.

As when a journey nearly done
    Some unforeseen event,
Some accident has counter run,
    Fruition to prevent.

But fears are banished when we hear
    That we're ahead of time.
Insurance money is the spear
    That keeps us back "on time."

But in "due time" the landing gained,
    The narrow streets all filth,
The ancient tiles by time so stained,
    With here and there much wealth;

The sudden endings of the streets,
    Scarce room to turn aside
From donkey cart which one meets,
    Or hurrying man beside,

Give variations to the trip,
    Lend vigor to the feet.
Marked changes these from life on ship,
    Or what at home we meet.

The hotel gained, refreshments had
    Out onward to depot.
See soldiers come—so poorly clad!
    But then nor cold nor snow.

But hurry on, the train soon starts,
    And should you miss it then
These loathsome, filthy, sickly parts
    Must prove two weeks your den.

Now safe on board the rickety cars,
    The whistle screams aloud,
  And off we go! My back! what jars!
    What jostlings! what a crowd!

The Isthmus now is halfway crossed,
    When suddenly a crack,
A jumping, tearing noise now tossed
    Our tender off the track.

The train is stopped, no damage done
    To life or limb of man;
But we must wait the setting sun
    To bring relief—what plan?

A telegram is straightway sent
    To Panama for aid,
And restless passengers consent,
    And broken tender's laid

Beside the track, and on we go
    A few short miles I ween,
Where switch accommodates, you know,
    And rarest plants are seen.

Again we stop; a hamlet near
  Of quaint and strange abodes,
Set high on posts, with thatched roof sear,
  In files along the roads.

From these the natives now pour out,
  Surprised to see us stop;
Run here and there, begin to shout:
  " Good cakes!" "coffee" (mere slop)!

" Sweet oranges" and " chocolate!"
  " Bananas" and " cigars!"
With " mango apples"—yes, " so sweet!"
  " Pine apples!" O, my stars!

What won't they bring! Let's leave the train,
  One hour is far too long
To view this scene nor see them gain
  Small pittance for their song.

Then passengers to rest the back
  And time to while away,
Some follow down the curving track,
  Some in deep woods now stray.

How dense the forest round about!
  How hot the sweltering air!
Now nimbus shades; then sun beams out,
  With crystal raindrops there

On brush and fern and palm leaf wide.
  A strange wild scene is this:
Bright plumaged birds on every side,
  Insects swarm and serpents hiss.

Above the scream of wild baboon,
  Or bright-winged paraquet,
Steam whistle sounds, by far too soon,
  This scene not half done yet.

A fortnight though might prove too long,
   So all on board again;
The native's quaint, persuasive song
   Is hushed by moving train.

Now Aspinwall heaves into sight,
   With bluff, and fort, and trees;
But slowly now the shades of night
   Close round to obscure these.

But yonder see our ship! she steams,
   All ready to depart,
Awaiting us. Far out she seems!
   Perhaps she's made a start!

But no; here comes a smaller boat
   To take us from the train
To where the great ships easy float
   That plow this raging main.

Leaves Aspinwall in shades of night
 Dim outlines in the mind.
Its record too, not clear nor bright,
 On history's page we find.

LEAVING THE ISTHMUS.

NOW again we leave the shore,
    Rolling, tumbling on!
Not so placid as before,
    Nausea comes anon.

Fading now the distant land,
    Passing from the sight:
Soon 'tis gone, the thundering strand
    Clothed in darkest night.

What shall be our future fate
    Plunging in the dark?
Cross the sea? Too soon? Too late?
    Ah, man! why thus embark?

Fitness is in everything;—
   Emblems, could we see.
Thus the voyage that we sing
   Has its mystery.

Birth was in a mountain home,
   Love came with that birth:
Childhood's feet then fain would roam
   Near parental hearth.

Youth came: then desire to go
   Roving further round;
Smooth Pacific seemed to show
   All youth's pleasure found.

All then tranquil as youth's dream,
   Not a care nor storm;
No anxiety 'twould seem
   Stirs the youthful form.

Calmly o'er this sea we sailed
    Pleased with every sight.
Landing gained—strange scenes availed
    Manhood's dawn to light.

Isthmus crossed—to manhood's prime,
    Brief though it may seem;
Surely comes a working time,
    Life's not all a dream.

Enter it with doubt and fear,
    Darkness supervenes,
Ups and downs through many years'
    Stormy billows—scenes

Trying oft the soul of man,
    As these billows test
Through each ship the workman's plan
    If it be the best.

A VOYAGE OF LIFE.

All through life wealth, fame, pursued
  Anxious labor brings,
Work and toil to be renewed
  Hoping better things.

WEST INDIES.

MORNING came on with a bright rising sun,
Soon to be hidden by gray clouds of dawn.
All seemed so different, so changed, not serene
Like voyage before the bright Isthmus so green.
The billows seem working, the clouds labor so,
To bring about something;—what is it? do you know?
Even ocean runs counter with current quite strong,
Instead of assisting our smooth course along,
As did blue Pacific some few days before,
When all seemed so quiet—e'en far distant shore.
This surging, this heaving, this motion, this strife;
This action among elements, thus teeming with life,

Fair emblem of manhood, its aims and desires,

Its striving, its hoping, to wealth it aspires.

The passengers also more active now seem,

Their staterooms are not half so pleasant they deem.

Their room-mates now strange, the captain is sought

To change them and rearrange all for naught,

He thinks, but listens to each in his turn;

Says everyone now by traveling must learn

That all is not comfort, annoyance must come

And slight inconvenience for leaving a home.

Thus sailing on o'er the sea islands appear,

Fresh and luxuriant, no leaf is now sear.

Slowly they come to us, come they so nigh

That trees and green bushes, with springs close by,

Invite us to come to them, share in their joy,

Peacefully wander, no strife to annoy.

"Come to us—come," they say; "lonely we be;

Long have we waited far out in the sea,
Something to offer to man's happiness;
Something to give him relief in distress;
Something, though small we be. Yes, we give all,
All to that wisdom which raises the pall
Of man's degradation, his ignorance and sin,
And bids heavenly sunlight his soul to shine in."
Slowly we pass them, and then to the sight
Dimly they vanish in gray, misty light.
Now comes proud Cuba, with forest of green,
Rising to Heaven, the dark clouds between.
Here is unrest, the clouds roll about,
The breakers run high, rough rocks pointing out
Obstruct them while striving the land to submerge;
The booming of waves thus sounding a dirge,
Deep-toned and soul-thrilling; its depths, oh, how
    deep!

It penetrates ocean and mountains so steep!
The rain is now falling far off on the land,
While here brightest sunshine encircles the strand.
High up in this mountain, which now seems so near,
In fancy the Mambi's voice signals we hear,
In tones ringing out to comrades far away,
Who catch them and listen,—they seem now to say:
"Valmasada!" "Valmasada!" What terror that name
To soldiers, and mothers and infants the same.
See parasites hanging from every tall tree,
Vines and thick undergrowth to shore of the sea.
No dwelling of man now fills the wild scene,
One mass of solid and beautiful green.
Man lives here, however, obscured from the world,
Not only by forests, but war clouds that hurled
Destruction and death on insurgents that roam
Through these mighty forests. No comforts of home,

No hallowing influence of civilized life,

Sheds peace and contentment on Mambi Land strife.

Independence they fight for, nor give o'er the task

Till liberty gained, in its sunshine to bask.

Without this they say exterminate foe

Or die in these woods that shelter us so.

But onward our gallant ship plows the deep main,

Nor stops at this little world looking to Spain

For care and protection, from foes without,

While foes from within now drive them about.

Slowly the land is now fading from view,

Yet still will our thoughts the Mambis pursue.

What shall we do for them? What can be done?

Who will take up the task? Who, when begun,

Will not assistance give downtrodden man?

Though dark his deeds may be, help him who can;

For redemption from oppression and wrong

Can be accomplished though the time be long.

Would man be brought from darkness to light?

Must he look upward, there all is bright.

Up to the source of all wisdom and love:

Up to the Savior, who came from above

To give a sample of what life should be,

To teach love and mercy and sweet charity,

Wisdom and mercy as boundless in extent

As stars throughout space in bright firmament.

A STRANGE PHENOMENON.

MANY days have come and gone,
 Many nights been dark,
Still we're sailing, sailing on,
 In our mighty bark.

Florida is far inland,
 Beaming forth the sun,
Stratus clouds on every hand,
 Noonday's heat begun.

Gray and filmy atmosphere,
 Thick and dense and warm;
Overhead the sun in sphere,
 Token of a storm.

Stillness—death was ne'er more still,
  Not a voice is heard,
Nor ship's engine seems to thrill.
  Ominous the bird

Lights him high on blackened arm,
  One shrill scream he gives;
Thus portentous of great harm
  To all on board that lives.

Surely now some scourge awaits,
  Say the sailors old;
Superstition thus relates
  Many legends bold.

Hark! again what sounds we hear
  Ringing through the air;
Bells and chimes ring out quite clear,
  Calling us to prayer

As in days of childhood gone,
    Heard we them before.
Mystery! they still ring on!
    Come they from the shore?

Is some phantom ship at hand
    Floating o'er the sea,
With the bells of childhood land
    Chiming harmony?

Or, the well-known village church
    Floating through the air?
Far o'erhead the haze we search
    Finding nothing there.

All delusion in the ear,
    Now 'tis still again!
Hark the echo far and near
    Ringing o'er the main!

Now dead stillness everywhere.
   See you lonely bird!
Black as night, sits high in air,
   No voice from him is heard!

Could it be—these sounds that float,
   These strange bells that ring,
Through the air came from his throat.
   Mystic song to sing?

Answer me, ye sailors, then,
   Living on the sea,
Is this strange phenomenon
   Still deep mystery?

QUARANTINE.

IN quarantine at last,
Old ocean's dangers past,
We are waiting for our ship's scourge to cease.
But great is our distress
For sickness and duress
Have robbed us now full many days our peace.

With bird and bells and chimes,
With heat and tropic climes,
Came smallpox to our vessel on her way.
The stricken soon we place
In life-boats swung in space,
Nor passengers could see them night or day.

A VOYAGE OF LIFE.

And now we're so near land

We see the pebbly strand,

Yet many days must linger ere our feet

Can kiss the welcome shore

As in the days of yore,

Or we our anxious friends again may meet.

But here comes a surgeon,

With vaccine he is urging

And compelling everyone to submit.

Like sheep they flee away,

Nor in his presence stay,

Yet every arm first bare is quickly hit.

The task is done he goes.

Relief from dreaded woes,

Of poisoned arms and tainted blood will come

With time, which brings release

From all that mars our peace,
Save death and separation in our home.

Behold the beauteous shore,
Far brighter than before,
For now beyond our reach it calmly lay,
Basking in the sunlight,
Forest, lawn and mansions white,
Forts, towns and cities scattered round the bay.

Here is life and action,
All in one direction—
That of gaining wealth, pleasure and renown.
All the world seems centered
In the port we've entered;
Busy throngs of vessels hurrying up and down.

The flags of all nations,
From way ports and stations,

Pass us as we lay in durance so long.
  Commerce coming, going,
  Small boats passing, rowing;
Grand excursions, lively music and song.

  Off for Staten Island,
  Grove and lawn and highland!
Merry people now free from toil and care—
  Joyous relaxation!
  Out from every station
Come the throngs to wander free in open air.

  Multitudes are coming,
  Business ever humming,
Drives them for a day to ramble o'er the hills:
  Some to seek enjoyment,
  Others base employment;
Others hear God's voice in music of the rills.

If language is to thought
What nature is to God,
And only can express one-half the real,
Then meadows, lakes and wood,
When fully understood,
Disclose much hidden wisdom—His ideal.

Strive upward to the source,
Let thought arise perforce
And pierce the very fountain of true light,
Then joy within is shed,
Nor conscience now is dead—
The soul is brought from darkness into light.

MOTIVES.

THIS world is all beauty
    And action and life,
Its pleasures, though fleeting
    And coupled with strife,
Are sweet to engage in
    Delightful the while.
Ah! who would not taste them
    The time to beguile?
But through them we're looking
    To something beyond,
Either soon to accomplish
    Or farther along,

To reap then the sowing;
  Now planting the seeds
That bring then the harvest
  Of all our good deeds.
In order iu this life
  That reaping may come
Many sow, toil and strife,
  Deserting a home.
Many sow, others reap,
  Thus gaining for naught
What they have not planted,
  Their labor not bought;
Thus changing enjoyment
  From where it belongs,
Nor reaping just merit
  Of many base wrongs.
We see them here reaping.

A VOYAGE OF LIFE.

The pleasures of wealth,
In luxury, grandeur,
   Forgetting the stealth
By which they have gained it,
   Not deeming the while
That conscience awakened
   Might pleasures defile.
Behold us surrounding
   A world of mankind,
Each seeking an object;
   Some daring to find
By means dark and hellish
   The aids to his end,
Not sparing the trust
   Of intimate friend.
Exertion like madness
   The motive that moves

All pleasures and business
    Along in their grooves.
With travel retarded
    By wave of the hand,
That bids us stay back,
    Nor deluge the land
With scourge or pestilence;
    For science says no!
Thus far shalt thou come,
    No farther shalt go.
But every thing earthly
    To end surely comes,
So quarantine ended
    Makes glad many homes.

Part 3.

STUDENT LIFE.

AH! who shall describe the student's gay life,
For here will we find all manner of strife!
Strife to be foremost in clinic and "quiz;"
Strife to be always "way up" in all "biz;"
Strife to delve deepest in medical lore;
Strife to be first at dissecting room's door;
Striving to see all that ever is seen;
Striving to "go for" the new students green.
Excelling each other in daring deeds
Of darkness not found in any the creeds.
Hazing in secret with plots that are dark;
Roving the city by night "on a lark;"

Visiting hospitals day after day;

Seeing the form divine nude as it lay

Dying or dead, as the case might be;

Mangled and bleeding or longing to flee

From suffering and sickness that can't be cured

But which old adage says must be endured.

Beguiling the soon to be benedict

From virtue, honor and constancy strict;

Leading him through many dens on Green street,

Till various potations make doubtful feet;

Taking him then to the home of his love.

Ah! could a Providence ruling above

Have so arranged it that she should be "out,"

Nor meet with him thus as he reels about!

But no! she answers the call of the bell,

And horror of horrors! dreadful the spell!

Five students, all strangers, save one dear face,

And this so changed!   See her eyes quickly trace
His dear manly form—not deeming the while
That comrades could thus her dear one defile.
How ended this episode no one of us knows,
For bidding adieu to them parlor doors close.
Four jolly students hie off in great glee;
Next morning a headache rewards their spree.
Darker deeds come anon, in jest begun,
Ending in tragedy, darkening the sun
With crime and balckness.   A demon seems bright
Compared to some intrigues that never see light.
In jest, apparently, two wills were made,
One by a student whose property laid
Far out in the West securely to stay,
In land and much stock, as he would oft say.
The other owned property here in New York
Worth many thousands—architectural work.

The will of the student ran thus in brief:
" At death, to my friend, my lands I bequeath
In view of his kindness, also a will
Made by him to me, this contract to fill."
The will of Mr.——, on the other hand,
" In view of friendship, and will about land,
Alike here bequeaths to this, my dear chum,
My estate on Third Avenue, now my home."
The student took his degree at Bellevue,
And then to his noble profession pursue
An office was rented in his friend's block,
With drug store beneath, and goods in full stock.
Soon the good landlord with some strange disease
Grew sick and then died his tenant to please.
In Sing Sing the jester languished till death
Freed him from murder by taking his breath.
And now, dearest reader, if nerves are quite strong

And equal the task we'll hurry along

And visit dissecting room.   Stop, do you say?

You can not endure it?   Well, turn away!

Turn over these pages nor read them until

Some change in the measure the lines shall fill.

If with me you go lay by the dread awe

Which filled your deep soul when dear one you saw

In death's cold embrace, for kindlier thought

Must now turn aside till science has wrought

A great preparation, which then will bring

Kindness and succor, relieving death's sting.

Despite my warning I see in your face

Indescribable thoughts, as onward we trace

Our steps a few blocks to East River's side,

To grand massive buildings, architects' pride,

Looming up silently, cold and still,

Emblems of secrets their sombre walls fill.

Your feelings more burdensome come as we climb
The wide and bright stairway. Dread you the time
When door shall be opened? Here, in we go!
Trembling? Apprehensive? Stop! you say? Oh!
This strange smelling odor, what can it be?
Softly you close then turn to see;
To follow so quietly, reverently on,
Through spacious apartment—other things gone.
Narrow long tables in rows through the hall,
With here and there charts that deck the white wall.
Brilliantly lighted by gas everywhere;
Groups of jets burning o'er each table there,
So nicely adjusted that motion is made
In each as 'tis needed no part to shade.
Hundreds are burning, students are working,
Each quite intently, seldom seen shirking
This, unto others, so loathsome a thing.

That thoughts of it shuddering disgust will bring.
Far down the centre four white walls are seen,
Forming, as it were, a dark room between.
But this room contains nor darkness, nor sprite,
But sheds to the lecture room floods of light.
Some tables are empty, many are used
By students in groups; some seem much amused,
Some chatting, some working, referring to books
With anxious, inquiring, perplexing looks.
Portions of bodies on tables around,
The work near completed much wisdom is found,
Of muscle, and tendon, and nerve, and brain:
Of bone and ligament, artery and vein;
Lymphatic and lacteal, pancreas and gall,
Ganglion and sinus, both great and small:
Of stomach and liver, kidney and lung,
And many strange things that can not be sung.
Here and there "new subjects," so pale and white,
With now and then one as black as the night.

See far in the northeast corner the place
Where cables and pulleys and black iron brace
Suspended from ceiling point out the source
Of some " material," you know, as of course,
The " morgue" is below. Ah! who would bequeath
His body to rise from the place beneath?
Smother these painful thoughts, if you can,
That rise in your mind for decaying man,
We'll turn and retrace our steps to the door,
Past tables and students, corpses and gore.
Students all smoking, working and reading,
Our coming and going scarcely heeding.
Some in dissecting gowns, others without,
But long linen dusters their legs about,
Reversed from the style of Grimes' coat—
Buttoned on the back, clear up to the throat.
Here a Professor " demonstrates" a brain,

There garrulous student makes tendon plain;
Others are joking over " too much fat,"
Talking of " hair grease," their " girls" and all that.
Condemn not too sternly the student's gay strife
Delving for principles thus to save life.
These jolly light spirits will soon become sage,
Give counsel in sickness to youth and old age;
Endanger their lives that of others to save,
Perhaps be laid low in premature grave;
Guard human life from pestilence and death,
Then heed lightly now what frivolity sayeth.

LETTERS FROM HOME.

BLEAK and cold with drifting snow
   Flying through the streets,
Quick the steps come to and fro
   Hurrying to their seats.
Students come from near and far,
   Now they hover o'er
Quaint steam heater,—iron bar
   Coiled above the floor.
Eagerly they first inquire,
   Letters may have come,
Loving words their work to inspire
   From dear ones at home.

Fair winged messengers of love,
    Dainty, white and neat,
Small inscriptions thus to prove
    Messages so sweet,
From "friend" and "lover," "sister" dear;
    Others also come
From father, mother—larger sear—
    Yet good news from home.
Welcome, aye, from Golden State!
    First to find its place
Came from "sister's" hand to greet
    A homesick, lonely face.
Feast his eyes on that dear sight!
    Ah! the joy it brings
Fills his soul with pure delight--
    Hopes of better things!
How he treasures pleasant thought!

How the bosom thrills!
All his labor goes for naught;
Bliss the future fills!
Solitude steals him away;
Anxiously he reads.
Hope seems almost led astray!
Heart with anguish bleeds.
Deemed he now that she would give
Some slight token sweet
Of her love;—bid his love live—
Hope again to meet.
Friendship only through the lines,
Gay and cheerfully,
Conversed as in olden times,
Happy, joyously.
Teaching school in forest wild,
Redwood trees among;

Happy now as any child
   In parental home.
Soon vacation days would come
   Then to Clear Lake fair
She would gladly gaily roam
   Through the pine wood air.
Then perchance familiar spot,
   Seeing once again,
She would not let be forgot
   " Brother's" scourge and pain.
Answered Sabbath afternoon;
   Household all were gone;
Stillness reigned in every room,
   Heart felt sad and lone.
No sound was heard save steady stroke
   Ticking loud and clear;
The clock alone the silence broke,

Musing to make dear,

By sweet associations past,

Of home and hallowed scene,

Of acts and looks too sweet to last,

Of love and joy serene.

Far away from home and friends

Her kind letters bring

Rays of hope—ample amends

For separation's sting.

Thus he wrote· "My sister dear,

None may truly know

Of the joy your letter gave

To me some days ago.

First it was of all the throng

Sent from Golden State,

Joyously it rushed along

Anxious eyes to sate.

Gladly I your well-known hand
   Recognized before
I had oped—to read began
   As in days of yore.
Pleasant voyage I have had,
   Strange grand scenes have viewed,
Now through work my spirits glad
   With bright hopes renewed,
Of eminence and much renown,
   Honor, fame and wealth,
Opportunities to crown
   Sickness and ill health
With vigor, strength and health restored.
   Happiness and joy
Bring from suffering much deplored
   Peace without alloy."
Thus the correspondence ran,

  Happy, joyously,
Scarce alluding to a plan,
  Not e'en cautiously,
Of what their future life might prove;
  Yet quite steadily
Grew a "sister's" "brother's" love,
  Sweetly, tenderly.
Fonder, dearer thoughts came now,
  Pure and holy love
Filled each soul though spoken vow
  Heard not God above.
How it charmed his soul to read
  Each thrice welcome line!
Every message brought the need
  Of others in due time.
Soon this happy intercourse
  Of thought and soul a part

Pierced a fountain at its source
    That flowed from heart to heart.
Ah, ever flow, holy stream,
    Bring peace and joy and bliss,
Fill up the soul beauteous dream
    Nor fruition miss!
Love that springs from God of Light,
    Pure, undying love,
Let no darkening shades of night
    O'er thy current move.
From thy source no shade will come,
    Naught can check thy flow—
Nothing but hell's fiends that roam
    Darkens thee below.
When we reach thy source, Oh, love!
    In that home of light—
Beauteous stream, the throne above,

Flowing ever bright—
We will know thy ecstasy,
All thy bliss so sweet,
All thy perfect constancy,
Loved ones there we'll meet.

ACROSS THE CONTINENT.

GRADUATION near at hand;
   Ah, bright, honored day!
   Proudest day among life's sand—
   Ne'er to fade away!
Now there came a promise sweet,
   Spoken timidly.
Ah! the joy when they should meet!
   Hope rose buoyantly.
Now he knew that far away
   One fond heart with joy
Waited the eventful day
   Soon its love to cloy.

Honor from the college given,
  Though so sweet to bear,
Sank before the sunlight driven
  From a scene more fair.
Day when love's work should be crowned,
  Happy hearts should meet;
Ever after love abound,
  Pure, serene and sweet.
Now farewell to college halls,
  Take its honors due,
For the world for workers calls,
  Workers tried and true.
Go ye forth in various ways,
  Where the world has need,
Go, and by your actions praise
  Them that sowed good seed.
Go and work for fellow man,

A VOYAGE OF LIFE.

For yourself the while;
Raise him up where e'er you can,
Nor yourself defile.
Now prepared for faithful work
By the training had,
Go, nor ever duty shirk
Though through misery led.
Duty done to man and self
Leisure comes with ease,
Many volumes from the shelf
Serve the mind to please.
Ever deem it wise to delve
Still for hidden truth,
Ever elevating self
Like ambitious youth.
Then shall come success in life,
Home and friends and fame,

Happiness, though tears and strife
  Mingle with the same.
Tears will purify the heart,
  Strife will make you bold,
Well in life to act your part,
  Not, indifferent, cold.
Come, then, contest with the world!
  Come what will or may
With your banner, truth, unfurled
  You will gain the day.
Truth, Ah! holy bright ensign!
  Wave thou ever o'er
Every motive of mankind,
  Every eye before.
Hurriedly some volumes bought,
  Instruments also,
Then a ticket office sought,

A VOYAGE OF LIFE.

Now prepared to go.
Cross the Continent by rail,
Less than seven days
Ere a loved one he should hail.
How the fancy plays!
Up the Hudson River fair,
Ah! how grand the sight!
Soft delightful evening air,
Shading into night.
Sing Sing first, then Albany,—
Rochester is here,
Crossing now Niagara,
Swinging in the air.
On he speeds, nor stops to view
This most wondrous scene,
Brighter thoughts and ever new
Fill the mind serene.

Now Detroit with floating road
    Bursts to view anon;
Wondrous ferry—such a load—
    It bears the train along!
Rain in torrents has submerged
    All the country round;
Swollen streams with terror urged
    Fence and drift along.
Cautiously we slowly move,
    Fearing accident;
Flooded bridges lest should prove
    Our great detriment.
Finally we cross the track
    Of wind storm and rain;
Swiftly now with "clickity clack"
    On we speed again.
Reached Chicago, time behind,

Just one hour too late;
Two through trains a day on time
To Nebraska State.
Over prairies vast and green:
Passing forest now;
Skirting clear meandering stream,
Under green hill's brow.
Towns and cities come and go;
Cornfields like the sea,
Waving in the winds that blow,
Pass us rapidly,
Houses scattered here and there
On the farms display
Scenes of home life everywhere.
Here a school at play!
Seems the teacher anxiously
Waiting here this train?

Possibly!—Quite certainly
   One beyond the plain
Waits, afar in mountain home,
   Soon with joy to greet
One no more from her to roam.
   Come, Oh, day so sweet!
Council Bluffs and Omaha
   Come and disappear.
Wilder scenes with strange dread awe
   Fill the mind with fear.
Antelope and buffalo
   Try with us their speed,
Wolves and Indians come and go,
   Scarce our presence heed.
Railroad track and telegraph
   All we have left here,
Marks of civilizations path

O'er the plains so drear.
Now the Rocky Mountains climb,
    Higher yet ascend;
Slower now, and yet on time
    Will our journey end.
No! "down breaks" the whistle screams!
    Ah! how short we stop!
Too much rain and swollen streams,
    A land slide from the top
Of yon high mountain covered o'er
    And destroyed our track;
Eight long hours suspense we bore
    Torture of the rack!
Grand the scenery round about,
    Yet no eyes had we
To enjoy; though cliffs jut out
    High and threateningly.

On we move when road repaired,
    Cañons tunnels through,
Scarce for meals or sleep we cared,
    Everything so new.
On, and on, and on, we speed!
    Salt Lake hurries by.
On we go! but now give heed—
    It comes so soon—'tis nigh!
Now we stop!—white tents all round
    Through the sage brush green.
Here a few days since was found
    A bright, triumphant scene;
East shook hands with youthful West,
    Gladly both displayed
Much good will;—with "spike" the best
    Here was "last tie" laid,
Binding us with iron bands

A VOYAGE OF LIFE.

  Stronger than the thread
That swings in air o'er our lands
  Bearing thought o'erhead.
On again, and ever on,
  Sleepy now and tired;
Rest awhile and wake anon—
  Snow-sheds have been fired;
Burning brightly through the pines.
  Tunnels dark again;
Then beyond the wood's confines
  To Sacramento's plain.
Now the city heaves in sight,
  Welcome place so gay;
Holiday begins to-night—
  Independence day.
Happy faces fill the streets,
  Joy fills many hearts;

Each the other gladly greets.
    Soon a horse race starts;
Some to-day to try their speed
    Came into the town,
Since the Sabbath brought the need
    Two days' sport to crown.
Some now celebrate the third,
    Others will the fifth,
Thus to reverence the word
    Given in Holy Writ.

Part 4.

HOME.

BRIGHTLY the sun shone in fair mountain town;

Joyously came he his love's work to crown;

Gladly she welcomed him home from afar.

Oh! holy dawn of hope, bright morning star!

Shine ever clearly while guiding their bark

Over life's rough sea, through the storms that are dark!

O! come now, sweet muses, inspire thou my song!

Fill every measure as time floats along!

Friends have now gathered to witness a scene

Which God has ordained sublime and serene;

Has given His sanction in words from above,

Ever uniting such hearts as may love.

Homestead is brightened, relations all here;
Dear friends have gathered from far and from near.
Bridesmaids selected from old friends and true
Fondly prepare her for scene ever new.
Gladly the time passes by on fair wings;
Sweetly they converse as each moment brings
Some added beauty to toilet and room,
Flower and ornament and sweetest perfume.
Sweeter than perfume each heart full of love
Sends a glad stream forth its source from above;
A stream whose clear ripple, so pure and so bright,
Uniting, o'erwhelms these two hearts with delight.
Fondly yet sadly the mother is seen
Coming and going bright faces between.
Ah! who can know of a fond mother's thought,
Seeing her child from the cradle thus brought
Through many long years of toil and of care

To hallow such scene so bright and so fair?
Far more who can know the feelings that swell
The soul of the child in this anxious spell?
Sad joy brings the thought that to-day she must leave
The home of her childhood, others receive
As friends and acquaintances; thus new life
Is brought to her now with that strange word wife.
"What shall my future be?" says she the while.
Musingly, silently—ever a smile
Hiding the turbulent depths of the soul,
Where gladness and joy with regrets now roll.
Great is the sacrifice which she has brought;
Home and dear schoolmates all go for naught.
Brothers and sisters' society gone—
All she surrenders for love's dearest boon.
Trusting in love she now ventures to stray
Over life's sea to sail gladly away.

Longer or shorter the voyage may be—
Terminate safely or disastrously.
Love be thy compass, oh, pilot, to guide
Safely past deep hidden rocks that betide
These voyagers dangers or suffering sore;
Land them, oh, pilot, on the evergreen shore!
Their voyage shall end not till death comes on
Bringing the passengers into their home,
Off from life's ocean whose waves ever roll
Bearing to eternity each living soul.
What shall eternity be when they land?
Bright home of beauty with welcoming strand?
Or shall it be darkness encircling the shore
With torture and torment for evermore?
Cheerfully, gaily the hour arrives
For blending in one these two loving lives.
Pastor and friends and relatives here,

A VOYAGE OF LIFE.

Soon in the distance three others appear;
One seems quite pensive, yet joy fills his heart
Knowing from loved one no more he shall part.
His soul fills with bliss as he thus draws near.
Never can man know these feelings so dear
Until they have moved his soul with delight.
They come like the rainbow of promise bright,
Shedding new glory on future and past.
Ah! may not this glory forever still last?
Glad is their meeting no more to sever;
Happy in love's fond presence forever.
Slowly the words came from depths of the heart,
"What God has united let man never part."
Gladly and happily hie they away
From childhood's roof, nor ever heard say
Regret at the going, for life seemed so new
Since love and happiness filled each day through.

Joyfully, cheerfully life is begun;
Hopefully, brilliantly rises the sun
Of promise and love to brighten their day,
Shed joy and happiness over their way.
Love rules supreme every act and each word,
With passions controlled no discord is heard.
Soon the new home seems dearer than the old,
For every day brings a new joy untold.
Working and toil bring sweet rest and repose,
Hallowed the scene when each day's labors close.
Influence of lotus comes on till the morn
Brings again labor their lives to adorn.
As oft through the day their loving eyes meet
Work is now rendered by each look more sweet.

HAPPINESS.

IF happiness, perchance, may be desire
And its fulfillment, then what joy bursts forth
To view again those scenes made dear by love.
Where hope and fancy bright in former years
Made glad the heart to think of what might be.
Ah! now rejoice with love's fond dream matured
And all that fancy painted realized!
What else could add to earthly bliss? What else
But ever new desire for something more
To share with those we love, and in its glad
Fruition see new joy in loved one's face?
With every added joy that comes and goes
With happy memory of its pleasing flight

There comes anon capacity for more;
Be they the joys and sweets of home, or be
They other forms of so-called happiness.
Then hearken now, give ear receptive mind,
And of the joys that come drink deep and long
From such as seemeth pure, and just, and true,
And lovely, honest and of good report.
New home, how sweet thy quiet pleasures are
When first with loved and loving hearts we come
To taste thy joys so new and strangely sweet!
When loving hands, in sweet accord with all
Our happy thoughts and voices, deftly place
Each ornament and picture on the wall;
Glad with approval and the sweet response
Of love from out the only soul we love.
Oh! new made, dearest, sweetest, lovely home,
Where two hearts join in all they say and do

To render all thy scenes more beautiful
And add new joys to each succeeding day!
Come days, and weeks, and months, and years, and all
Thy joys thus multiply. But cares of those
In deep distress and sickness came, and yet
With their relief from darker woes of death
Came ever to the hearts in this new home
Glad thoughts of duty done.
Thus many years of love and pleasure ran,
Each in a sphere where duty called most loud,
Where act of love and kindness could be done,
Or skill to save from death could be bestowed.
She glad to benefit mankind, or raise
The darkness from a faltering, sinning soul
And point it to an everlasting home.
While he to save the mortal part from death
Gave time and toil and sleepless, stormy nights.

She watches anxiously with wakeful eyes
Within the lonely cottage window there.
Aroused at every noise to see him come
From out the dismal, dark and rainy night
Where he had gone to succor dying man.
No sleep she knows till coming break of day
Has brought return of him she loved and watched.
Such separations and such dread suspense,
Though short in time to others they may seem,
Yet seem they now to her as endless pangs
That pierce the soul with strange anxiety.
With depth of love comes corresponding woe
At separation from the soul we love.

SADNESS.

THERE came a day
When deeper anguish rolled across her soul.
When all alone in midst of books she loved,
With husband on his errands of relief,
A crimson, vital and yet deathly fount
Leaped forth from out that throbbing, loving breast.
Too well she knew its import. And though small
The stream that seemed so bright, she realized
That what she oft had dreaded now must come.
The husband soon returned; his well-known step
She heard, but dare not move his face to greet

At welcome door, as was her gladsome wont,
For fear her life-blood forth again should spring.
The fond embrace—then tears, ah, bitter tears!
Filled loving eyes, while thus she gently spoke:
"My darling, I must leave you soon—for see—
See this—consumption's never failing mark
Has come to tell us we must surely part.
How soon we know not, yet you know 'twill come
That I must go and be with you no more.
Oh, darling! can I go and leave you thus
Alone in life?"
With words he knew were false he thus replied:
"My dear, think not too sadly of our lot,
This hemorrhage is small and doubtless will
Relieve the slight congestion of the lung
Produced by taking cold some weeks ago."
But deep within his anguished soul he knew

Far better than his words which scarce deceived.

Some months were passed and with them came return

Of that dread symptom, many others too

That told too plainly of disease within.

Then May time came with plans for mountain trip

To early scenes 'mid lakes and well-known woods.

Where love was born. Thus seeking to restore

The waste begun, and if perchance to check

The onward march of that which yet to skill

Bids stern defiance.

Amid these old familiar mountain scenes

She moves again with troubled, sorrowing soul.

Some dear, familiar faces she now meets,

But many gone leave aching voids within

For friends of early days.

    How sad she feels to see

At door of death the honored, manly brow

Of one she knew in former years—her pride
As pupil—bright-eyed boy. But sadder still
To know the self same hand, that dread disease
Of which he dies, is even now at work
In her pale form, and soon—too soon—must she
In like condition pass from earth away.

   The pure and fragrant mountain air
Brought scarce a change. And with the Autumn came
Return to home and husband dear. With sad
Farewells—ah, last farewells—to friends of youth
And relatives so dear, she turns her face
Towards one bright spot of all the earth to her
Most dear;—that new made home where love
And tenderness abides; where anxious heart
To her so dear awaits to welcome her.
She's coming home to die! O, God of love,
And power, and might, is there indeed no help?

O, God! my God, canst Thou not save
  All them who to Thee cry?
Hear me, my Father, as I crave
  Succor from Thee on high,

To check what man with all his skill,
  And all he knows of Thee,
Can not arrest or change at will
  From wasting tendency.

My God, I've sought Thee in Thy laws,
  Through Nature traced Thy power,
The defects of my race its flaws,
  My watchword many an hour.

Yet still I come, when all else fails,
  To Thee my source of light,
And ask and pray with many wails
  That morn shall not be night

Canst Thou not hear my feeble cry?
  O, God, I scream to Thee
For help! Oh, help me or I die!
  Oh, save my own to me!

She has sought health in other climes,
  Now, guided by Thy laws,
She's coming home—I hear sad chimes.
  Oh, save from death's dark jaws!

Thou canst arrest this slow decay,
  Thy word and laws proclaim.
Wilt Thou not in her case display
  Some token of thy aim?

Oh, show by this Thy power supreme
  O'er man, though science guide!
Show love to triumph, love sweet theme
  Through Christ, the crucified.

" How glad I am to be at home again!
What pleasant and refreshing rest I'll have!
So tired I've been these many weary months,
And longed so much to be with you once more.
I'll never leave you, darling one, again,
Until I go where you must one day come.
I'll stay with you a few short weeks or months
And then I'll go away again; no more
To be with you in this our pleasant home.
Do not weep, for if it be God's will
Then must it be for our own good."

      What torture to the living, loving soul
Can equal that which comes to those who see
A loved one—ah, one's better self—for days,
And weeks, and months, to suffer and draw near
The verge of that mysterious, bournless land
Beyond the tomb? When as each day brings forth

Its busy cares and duties to be done,
The mind is almost lost in earnest toil.
And so engaged in its absorbing work
That future cares scarce penetrate the thoughts;
Then as the homeward footsteps gladly traced,
How like an avalanche breaks o'er the mind
The thought that death is lingering in our home!
Nor will his waiting e'er give o'er until
He takes a dearly loved one from our sight.
Ah! thou dread terror of the human mind,
Unwelcome monster, wilt thou e'er remain?
Oh! that I could but summon heaven and hell,
And all the mighty powers that in them be,
And all of earth and men that show forth might,
How far would I not banish thee from sight,
And thus restore my home to what it was
Before thou camest, with sneaking, stealthy tread

A VOYAGE OF LIFE.

To mock my skill and scorn my aid of men!
He further, mocking, says: " Be not enraged,
Thou caust not drive me hence. I came for her
And she must surely go. I care not aught for thee
With all thy skill; nor all of man combined;
His boasted science; or the aid of thy
Most skillful brethren of the healing art.
Yes, bring them on, use every means now known,
And yet thou soon shalt see I'll gain the day,
And bear her hence into my doorless house."
Ah! thou grim monster, wilt thou ever mock
And thus deride my grief? Thou shalt be gone;
She loves not thee but me. She fain would stay,
And she must stay. Begone, thou fiendish king
Of terrors, from my former happy home!
Then through the skill of various minds, and by
The power of love, and strong desire to live,

The pale, fair form would seem new strength to gain
And thus new hopes arouse within the breast
That possibly the monster now had flown.
Then home was joyous once again, for now
Bright hope lent buoyancy to every act
And o'er each scene of home shed rays of gladness.
Could this continue what a joy 'twould bring!
Ah! sweet it is indeed to conquer foe,
But sweeter far when mighty is that foe
And ever seeks our homes to desecrate!
But then that daily, hollow, wearing cough
Told but too plainly of the secret foe
That lurked and e'en abode within the room,
And only hid himself away from sight
When love and hope would fain not see his form.
Ah! come thou forth from out thy hiding place,
Destroyer of my earthly happiness,

And meet me face to face, that I may hurl
Thee hence so far that thou canst ne'er return!
All vain attempts to dispossess him of
His lovely, fading prize—he only scoffs,
And still remains.
At length when days, and weeks, and months have
    passed
His form familiar grows. He hovers round
The sleeping couch, and totters by the side
Of his pale victim, as she comes and goes
With feeble step from room to room.
    When oft returned
From busy toil and care, the husband sees
The wasting form, to shun death's presence dire,
Has left the dreaded sick room bed, and now
Reposes where new life perchance may come
In gentle sleep; nor now disturbed by him

Whose quiet footstep hurries to her side;
He ever finds the reaper hovering o'er;
His fingers playing with her shining hair,
And fondly pressing the unconscious cheeks
That ne'er return to wonted fullness more.
While every impress of unwelcome touch
Marks that fair face death's own. Unconscious still
She sleeps. The bony reaper with a hand
Uplift, as if to warn him cautiously
Away, says: "Stop! do not come near; disturb
Not this her sweet repose, nor me in this
My tender care for her. I love to be
Thus near to her, and to behold these cheeks
And rosy lips which you so oft have kissed
Grow pale and lean. I love to think the while
That soon—yes, very soon—she'll go away
With me and never more return to you.

This face, though pale, will look so sweet within
Its beauteous casket all bestrewn with flowers;
These hands so white then folded o'er this breast
Then cold will never more grasp yours in love;
This mind now in such sweet and calm repose
Will then respond to none of your sad grief;
These eyes then closed as now will never more
Beam forth the joyous love that fills her soul.
Ah! contemplate with tears my lovely prize!
For see e'en now how much like me she looks,
Save this too rapid breathing, heaving breast.
But see! she startles; I will disappear
Lest she should see me watching o'er her now.
Remember this in all your converse sweet
With her, that she is mine, no longer thine."
"Ah! darling, is it you? I've been asleep.
Such peaceful and refreshing sleep! Perhaps

It was not sleep—I hardly know—for see,
I'm rested now and feel quite strong again.
If this were sleep then could I always be
In such condition. Shall I say I dreamed,
Or was it something more? Ah! surely more;
For such a rest I ne'er before have known.
The Savior took me in His loving arms
And bore me as a child throughout His Home.
At first I thought the arms were yours, and then
Such beauty ever filled my wondering eyes
That well I knew and felt no earthly scene
Could thus my soul with bliss and rapture fill.
There in His Father's House a mansion fair
And beautiful I saw prepared for us.
Its holy grandeur tongue can ne'er express,
Nor its perfection for our happiness.
Oh! darling, this our earthly, happy home,

Though dear and pleasant as a home can be,

Seems nothing when compared to what I saw.

I now can go content to leave you here,

For well I know that you will one day come

To this our second new made, glorious Home,

And be again with me forever there."

The weeks rolled on and brought the merry May;

But sadness teemed in every leaf and flower

To him who realized that now had come

The time when all these bright and fragrant flowers

No more could charm the wasting form, save as

They came from loving hands and tender hearts

Of friends to decorate the sick one's room.

Ah, loving hands! what joy these flowers bring

To soften sadness with their fragrance sweet!

They speak of weeping hearts that fain would bring

Relief from suffering, and restore to life

The object of their kind solicitude.

How sad to know that as these fragrant flowers

Are offered, each with sympathy and love,

From hearts that feel what they can not express,

The soul that lingers for a few short days

Responds with love as deep and pure, and sweet,

As that of angels; for she now seems one,

Waiting only for the time to come

When life's rough sea, now calm as after storm,

Shall bear her gently to the heavenly shore,

Which she now sees and anxiously awaits.

Oh! happy landing after voyage done,

That has been oft beset with danger and

With torturing doubts! Yes, joyous it may be

To worn and weary voyagers. But Oh,

The bitter anguish of the loving hearts

That see them go! It seems as if pale death

Were ever passing through earth's garden, full
Of living and immortal, precious souls,
And gathering of the brightest, fairest flowers,
And ever making fragrant, lovely wreaths,
And bright bouquets, with which to decorate
The heavenly throne.
O, restless, suffering, anxious, torturing hours,
Before the spirit bids a last farewell
To earth, and friends, and home, and loved ones dear!
What language can the depth of anguish tell
That fills each soul, as round the dying couch
They gather from afar to bid a last
Farewell? O, weeping hearts, will ye not burst,
So full of tearless, suppressed grief ye seem?
Could tears but flow perchance t'would give relief.
But no, they must not come as yet.
    The night grew slowly on,

And with it came that last, sad awful scene.

The restless, sleepless yet angelic eyes

Gave token of approaching death; of that

Last sleep which never more a waking knows.

All present felt it coming o'er her now.

And she, whose wakeful eyes for days no sleep

Had known, felt too that now sweet sleep would come.

She knew—ah, yes, too well she sadly knew—

That she must now a long and sad farewell

To friends and sister, brother, husband give.

O, can it be that she must go away?

Will not my God give rescue from the scene?

Will not my brethren of the healing art

Save her a few days more to be with me?

"My darling, do you think I'm dying now,

Or is it only sleep that makes me feel

More comfort now than I for days have felt?

No pains, no restlessness, nor dread I feel.
I must be dying, surely—am I not?
Dear sister, do not cry. Bring baby here;
His auntie loves him so. He little knows
How sad I am to leave him thus before
His memory can in after years retain
Fond thoughts of me. How happy you will be
With him when he is grown. Will you not then
Recall how much I love him now? And how
I hope and pray, with this my dying breath,
That he may be a great and useful man
And learn to know how much I loved him?
My only sister, well I know—too well—
How lonely you will be when I am gone,
For Ma has left us all alone! But then
You know she was so good and kind to us
That we will one day find her where she's gone—

And I will very, very soon be there.
My brother, I shall soon be gone from you;
Oh, will not you so live that you may come
Where Ma and I will wait for you?
My darling husband, you will come I know,
If you will only true and faithful be.
You love me, do you not? My love for you
Has been so great that I could never give
You up to go away and leave you here
Alone. I often hoped that we might go
Together to the other happy home
Which Jesus has so well prepared for us.
What will you do, my darling, when I'm gone?
These rooms will be so sad and lonely then.
Will you stay here or will you go away?
Kiss me good-by, for I am dying now.
Do not cry so!—It is not hard to die."

Then came that perfect rest. It was not sleep
But death, which once before had been so near.
The lips moved gently as in trusting tone
Of whispered words she spoke to One, whose voice
None heard save she who rested in His arms,
And as His words fell gently on her ear
She seemed to listen so attentively
That husband hovering o'er her dying face
Heard her in earnest whispers to converse,
Make this request of Him with whom she spoke:
"You will take care of husband, will you not?"
Then waiting briefly as if for reply
With anxious look until she heard it come;
Then pleased as though a doubt had been removed,
As if a promise had to her been given.
She spoke aloud to those who wept around,
In tone betokening confidence and love,

Assuring him from whom she now must part
That " Jesus will take care of you."
Then all was still; the gentle spirit borne
Away within the arms of tenderness
And boundless love, left sobbing, bleeding hearts
To drink at deep affliction's bitter fount,
Its waters ever adding to the thirst,
Until they drink, and weep, and drink again.
Now overcome with weeping fall to sleep,
Then wake to weep again, and still again
To moan through shades of sorrow's darkest night;
To dream and then awake to know the worst,
And wonder if it can be truly so
That all indeed of life and hope is gone.
Now darkest blackness falls around o'er earth;
And morn seems night, though brightly now the sun
Beams forth, as if to make the darkness of

These weeping souls yet still the more intense.

Above these bitter waters stands the throne

Of mercy, ever beaming brightest rays

For every weeping, bleeding, stricken heart.

And though such hearts but seldom see its gleam,

Yet now a little ray, with kindly light,

Beams through the darkness to one stricken soul

And bids it hope. And now he truly sees

That fair and lovely face, so cold in death,

Is not the recent sufferer of her ills

But his fair bride, as fresh and beautiful

As when they first were wed.

          He further knows

That in her Father's House a mansion fair

Is now her happy home. That there with love

Which never dies she waits and watches still

His coming, as in days forever gone.

www.ingramcontent.com/pod-product-compliance
Lightning Source LLC
Chambersburg PA
CBHW030311170426
43202CB00009B/960